The Relaxed Rabbit

The Relaxed Rabbit

Massage for Your Pet Bunny

Chandra Moira Beal, RMT
&
Maia

iUniverse, Inc.
New York   Lincoln   Shanghai

The Relaxed Rabbit
Massage for Your Pet Bunny

iUniverse, Inc.

For information address:
iUniverse, Inc.
2021 Pine Lake Road, Suite 100
Lincoln, NE 68512
www.iuniverse.com

This book is written with the intention of helping pet guardians develop a stronger bond with their animals. It is imperative to understand the health conditions and personality of your pet before attempting massage. These instructions are meant to be used with animals with which you are familiar. Please pay careful attention to the contraindications and cautions inserted throughout the book. The author assumes no responsibility for any injuries as a result of the information contained herein. This book is not meant to diagnose, treat, or cure any medical problems, nor is it meant as an alternative to proper medical care. Please consult your veterinarian with any questions about your pet's health, and use common sense when applying massage techniques.

Anatomy illustrations from The Laboratory Anatomy of the Rabbit, C.A. McLaughlin and R.B. Chiasson, 1990, reproduced with permission of The McGraw-Hill Companies

ISBN: 0-595-31062-1

For Maia

My Familiar Friend

CONTENTS

ACKNOWLEDGEMENTS

Any book is the culmination of great ideas from great minds. Thanks to Yasmin Jackson for encouraging me to write this book, and helping with editing; to the folks at the House Rabbit Resource Network in Austin, Texas for teaching me about rabbits from the beginning; to Kim Meyer for photography and proofreading; to Dawn Canelones and Bugsy for posing for photographs; to Todd Riggan, DVM for supporting Maia throughout her life and for reviewing this book; to Peggy Lamb for teaching me human massage so I could share it with animals; to Jorja Latham for editing; to Kathy Beal for help with the cover image; to Gallagher for last-minute modeling; and for all the people who took me seriously when I shared this idea with them.

Special thanks to Kathy Smith for helping me make this dream project a reality.

And, of course, thanks to Maia for her countless hours of patient teaching, and for being my "guinea pig."

A NOTE FROM MAIA'S VETERINARIAN

The benefits of massage have been known for ages, but this practice has only recently been applied to our pets. As our animals have become family members, we have introduced many services and benefits to them. Pet massage is just as relaxing for our animals as it is for us. Massage can help strengthen the bond between you and your special friend, as well as help tissues heal.

The applications for pet massage are numerous and can serve for aching muscles, arthritic conditions, relaxation, trauma or injuries, and to aid in healing post-surgically. There are numerous intangible benefits to massage. The combining of your energies creates the unique relationship that you both experience. It can increase one's awareness of their surroundings and put them in touch with senses they may not have been aware of.

In this book, Chandra Beal shows you how to achieve these benefits with your own pets. As a specialist in rabbit medicine, I can attest first-hand to the positive effects massage had on Maia and other rabbits who received regular therapeutic touch.

In this time of preventative medicine and wellness, massage meshes well in our psyche. It has a strong place in veterinary medicine because of its healing and bonding powers. Massage can open our minds and hearts, broaden our horizons, and increase our awareness. It is rewarding to see the benefits of massage in a happy tail wag or satisfying purr. I recommend this book as a great place to start your own healing journey alongside your pets.

Todd Riggan, DVM
White Rock Veterinary Hospital
Pflugerville, Texas
info@whiterockvet.com

AUTHOR'S PREFACE

This book is a dream come true. It is the culmination of three passions in my life: writing, massage, and rabbits.

I worked as a freelance nonfiction writer for many years, writing for magazines and self-publishing books. After a mini-lop named Maia entered my life, I began writing about pet care and rabbits in particular. I got involved in numerous animal welfare organizations. In 2001 I decided to pursue my dream of going to massage school, and I opened my practice in 2002. Maia supported me through all these endeavors, inspiring me to write about her antics and allowing me to practice massage strokes on her.

I massaged Maia intuitively from the day she hopped across the threshold. It simply felt good to pet her, and she seemed to enjoy it. I found myself enjoying great health benefits just from being with her; I was more relaxed, happier. Current research supports the animal-human bond as a powerful healing tool. I noticed that Maia endured illnesses that had been difficult for other rabbits, and that she recovered quickly from stress. Her tissue felt different from other rabbits the same age and breed.

I began to take notice of the tangible effects of massage on us both, and wondered how to share our knowledge with the world. It wasn't until I was part way through massage school that I started formalizing the techniques and routine. It seemed only logical to call upon my writing experience and produce a book about it.

Within these pages I share what I learned by trial and error. I spent many hours with my hands on Maia, following my intuition. I studied rabbit anatomy and tried to adapt Swedish massage techniques to rabbits. I listened to Maia for feedback and developed a routine that covers the whole body. I use this as the groundwork from which to grow and evolve. Each session is slightly different and responds to the present moment. Learning to be in the present is a wonderful gift from our animal friends. I encourage you to try it!

Be creative and have fun. Massage can be profoundly spiritual as well as playful. It is my sincere hope that by sharing massage with your pets, you will both benefit from its healing effects, and that it will bring you closer to each other in the process. Blessings!

Chandra and Maia
Winter 2002
Austin, Texas

CHAPTER 1

What is Massage?

Massage is the touch of the physical and energetic body with a healing purpose, and a time honored method of reducing stress and tension. Most massage techniques involve hands-on manipulation of the muscles and soft tissues of the body. The techniques discussed in this book are taken from Swedish massage strokes that form the basis for most Western massage techniques.

Acceptance of massage as a viable therapy has increased over the last decade. Over one-fourth of American adults have now had a massage, as opposed to 10 percent in 1997. There is no reason that our animal friends should not share in the benefits of massage.

Animals engage in a form of massage in the wild—grooming. Many species lick their offspring after birth to stimulate physiological processes, and most orphaned animals do not thrive due to lack of touch. Scientific evidence documents the importance of touch to our ability to survive and thrive in life. Animal massage is now coming into its own as a proven support to pets' care.

Massage is great preventative medicine and an excellent way to support healing for both people and pets. It can help reduce stress and muscle tension, increase circulation of blood and lymph, strengthen the immune system, increase muscle tone, and expand range of motion. It can aid in recovery from injury and help to maintain overall health and muscle tone. For animals that are especially active or athletic, massage can help to increase flexibility, remove toxins from stressed muscles, and relieve muscle spasms.

Maia After a Massage

Why Massage?

Modern pets are often confined indoors and don't engage in the same sort of running and foraging activities that their wild counterparts do. This sedentary lifestyle can lead to obesity, lethargy, and lack of interest in life. Along with a healthy diet and exercise, massage can help bring vitality back to these animals.

Selective breeding and domestication have altered the structure of many species, such as the bulging eyes of the dwarf rabbit or the exaggerated ears of an English lop, and this can result in physiological stress. Massage can help alleviate some of these conditions.

Going beyond the physical benefits, massage is also helpful for emotional issues, and is a key element in re-socializing animals that have been abused or neglected. A caring touch speaks volumes and is often the first step in rebuilding trust. Research has shown that physical contact for an animal who is emotionally attached to a human is as rewarding as being given a favorite treat.

Massage can even help ease the stresses of daily life, such as a visit to the veterinarian. A rabbit who is used to being handled in a caring way will have a higher threshold for stressful situations and will take life in stride. This makes the caretaker's job easier when it's time to cut nails, give medications, or examine teeth. My own vet can attest to Maia's hind legs stretched out on the examination table. Daily massage over extended periods of time even boosts the immune system so that rabbits don't get sick as easily and can recover more quickly if injured.

By massaging your pet regularly, you can detect changes in their health immediately. Daily touch will you give you a baseline knowledge of what is normal for your pet, and can be a source of information about your pet's muscle condition and their overall health. While not a substitute for veterinary advice, massage is a low-cost, safe, and natural supplement to your pet's care. Massage has no harmful side effects; it is non-invasive and supports the body's own healing process.

Stroking a pet not only offers the animal touch that it desires and deserves, but can also ease the owner's stress. According to a study in Hypertension, 48 people involved in high stress occupations and who also had high blood pressure were asked to adopt a cat or dog along with taking the drug lisinopril. When the participants' responses to a stress trigger (math exercises) were tested in their home environment, those with a pet in the same room had a lower blood pressure reading than non-pet participants.

Another study at New York State University at Buffalo showed that subjects accompanied by their pets were less likely to have increased heart rate and blood pressure than those who were alone or with their spouses or friends.

Sharing massage with animals is a great way for us to learn about ourselves, and touching strengthens the animal-human bond.

Animal massage is a win-win prospect.

How Massage Works

The effects of massage are either reflexive, meaning that they indirectly stimulate the nervous system, endocrine system, and chemicals in the body; or the effects are mechanical, directly affecting the soft tissue or circulating fluids. Massage can do both.

Massage itself is an aerobic activity. While it increases circulation, it aids in not only the transport of oxygen to the tissue but the elimination of metabolic wastes and toxins from the muscles. This flushes muscles with nourishment and cleans them out so they can function optimally.

Muscles that have been overworked or underworked can create adhesions, literally places where they become "glued" or stuck to the surrounding tissues. Massage can help to break up these adhesions, allowing the muscles to function in the manner in which they were intended.

The typical house rabbit will benefit from regular, simple relaxation massage. This whole-body routine reduces stress and promotes relaxation. It can help break up scar tissue and speed recovery from injuries. It can tone muscles (tone is the natural firmness of the muscles and their readiness to respond to stimuli). Massage can reduce muscle spasms associated with daily stress, and provide better joint flexibility and range of motion. It can increase blood and lymph circulation. All these things lead to a healthier skin and coat, and a strengthened immune system. As your pet ages, these things will come into play. Start early to build the foundation of health for tomorrow.

What Massage is Not

Massage is considered an adjunct to other therapies. While it offers many benefits in and of itself, it is not a cure-all. Massage works best in conjunction with other healthy lifestyle changes such as a good diet and regular exercise.

While massage can help you become more familiar with your pet's health and overall condition, and make it easier to detect changes in their health, it is not a diagnostic tool by itself. If you suspect something is wrong with your pet, you should always consult your veterinarian. If you are taking your animal to a professional massage therapist, realize that they may not have all the answers. A responsible therapist will readily refer you to another professional if they feel it would be more beneficial for your animal. If in doubt, refer out!

Contraindications

There are situations when massage is contraindicated, or not recommended, because it can actually be harmful. In some cases, such as with a healing wound, you can work around the affected area, but still give a general massage. Use common sense.

It is important to consider your rabbit's health history before beginning massage therapy. Consider any past or present injuries they may have suffered. Are they taking any medications or supplements? Have they had recent surgeries? How will these circumstances interact with massage? If you have any doubts, ask your vet if massage is appropriate.

When to Avoid Massage:

- The animal just ate. Allow at least 30 minutes from the last snack. Since rabbits are grazers, use common sense here. No vigorous tummy massage right after they eat. But a neck rub after a few nibbles of hay is fine.

- Infection or disease. Massage can spread bacterial and other infections throughout the body. Let an animal get well before attempting massage. However, a simple laying on of hands or a friendly pet can help improve a sick animal's mood.

- Fever. Massage increases metabolism and circulation, which a fever has already accomplished.

- Pregnancy. Because pregnancy presents so many variables, it is best to avoid massage here. (Besides, your animal should be spayed or neutered to prevent overpopulation!)

- After intense exercise. Let the heart rate slow down before a massage session.

- Cancer and tumors. These can be spread through the lymphatic system by massage.

- Pain medications. These can desensitize your animal to deep pressure and you could inadvertently injure them.

- Diabetes. Massage affects metabolism.

- High blood pressure. Massage affects circulation.

You should also avoid massaging certain parts of the body called "endanger-ment sites." These are vulnerable parts of the body where you should avoid applying pressure:

- Eyes
- Carotid artery under the ears, chin, and neck
- Directly on the spine or vertebrae
- Over the kidneys
- Back of the knee
- Femoral artery (on the inside thigh)
- Abdomen (gentle abdominal massage is okay, but avoid deep pressure)

General Tips for Massage

- Always begin with light pressure and gradually increase the pressure. It is important to warm up the tissue before applying deeper work.

- When applying long effleurage strokes, follow the direction of the muscle fiber (see muscle chart for a general overview). Friction uses strokes across the "grain" of the muscle.

- Most massage strokes are directed toward the heart to encourage blood flow through the veins. The heart muscle pumps out blood into the body, while the arteries themselves contract to push the blood along. Think of a garden hose. If you apply pressure, it crimps and pressure builds up. When you release it, blood rushes back in. Blood flow depends on the contraction of the muscles against the veins, which are more superficial than arteries. However, most animals' fur grows away from the body, and many animals find it uncomfortable to have their fur rubbed the wrong direction. Adapt to your pet's tolerance and do what feels natural to you both.

- When making circular motions using any stroke, clockwise circles will have an increasing energy or stimulating effect, while counterclockwise circles lessen energy and are sedating. For example, if a rabbit is aggressive and has large knots between its shoulders, use counterclockwise circles. A rabbit who is lethargic could use clockwise circles.

- Try to feel the difference between superficial skin and muscle. Skin will slide easily over a muscle in a healthy animal. If you've ever given a rabbit a subcutaneous shot, you already know how to pull the skin away from the muscle.

- Use both hands. If necessary, stabilize the body with your opposite hand while you isolate and work out tension with the other.

- Try to maintain contact with the animal at all times during your session. This is reassuring and helps you stay focused and helps keep your pet relaxed. Imagine your hands moving the way water flows through a stream, in one long continuous motion.

- Watch your pet's reaction to touch. Notice her facial expression. Are her eyes closing? How is her breathing? Is it slow and even? Other signs that your pet is relaxing are sighs, stretches, snorts, and falling asleep. Perhaps she'll rest her chin on the floor in the submission stance, or pay you the ultimate compliment of chattering her teeth.

- Don't give up after the first few tries. Pets will quickly learn what to expect with your massage routine and will relax easily with your touch in time.

- Follow your intuition and trust your hands. Use this book's routine as a place to begin, then add in your own moves. Let your pet inspire you.

- Let your pet come to you when she is ready for massage. If she resists at all, don't push it. Always let the animal be in control of the session. If she leaves in the middle of it, let her go.

- It's important to center yourself before beginning a massage. Be aware of your own body and take long, deep, conscious breaths. Your own tension can be transferred to your pet, so take a few moments to breathe, stretch, and feel your feet firmly planted on the ground before you begin.

- Sanitation is important to prevent the spread of disease, especially when working with animals. Always wash your hands with warm, soapy water before and after the massage. Remove any dangling or sharp jewelry before starting the session.

- Massage time should be quality time. Turn off the phone, play relaxing music, turn down the lights…whatever makes it more relaxing for you both. Make massage a regular event and a magical bond will develop between you and your pet.

I'm So Relaxed!

CHAPTER 2

A Crash Course in Rabbit Anatomy

Rabbits are herbivores that serve as the prey of many carnivores in the wild. They are designed to eat frequently, live fast, and die young. Fortunately for house rabbits, their life span has greatly increased due to domestication, better medical knowledge about their species, and the fine care of their guardians. Still, modern rabbits are generally built like their ancestors.

There are some outstanding features of the rabbit as they relate to massage:

Rabbits have lightweight skeletons so they can sprint at high speeds. Their skeletons make up only 8-9 percent of their total body weight, which means that they are fragile and can easily suffer skeletal injuries if handled improperly.

A rabbit's hind legs should always be supported when held in your arms. Their largest muscles are in their hind legs so they can push off with force.

They have a near 360-degree field of vision with their eyes placed at the sides of the head, 190 degrees on each side, watching for predators.

The ears can rotate in several directions, by virtue of several intricate muscles, to take in subtle sounds.

Rabbits also have large, strong muscles in their jaws for gnawing and chewing plant fibers.

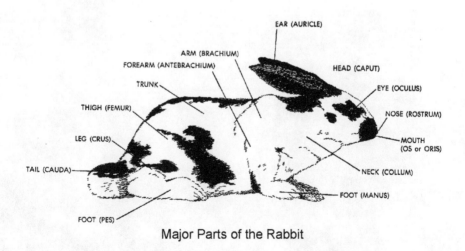

Major Parts of the Rabbit

Finding Bony Landmarks

To find our way around the muscles of the body, it is helpful to learn what are called "bony landmarks." These are points on the body where you can easily feel the skeletal system, and use it as a point of reference for locating muscles.

Skull

Hold your thumb and first finger at the tip of your rabbit's nose. Stroke the top of the head toward the ears and feel for two deep grooves alongside the nose. These points are where the nasal bones meet the incisive bones that hold the front teeth. Sinus pockets lie underneath. Rabbits' teeth are "open rooted," meaning their incisors grow throughout their lives. These grooves are where the incisor teeth begin to grow. Most rabbits love to be stroked along these grooves.

Keep sliding your fingers toward the ears over the frontal bone. Just above the eyes feel for a ridge called the supraorbital process. You generally want to avoid massaging the area under this ridge, close to the eye.

Rub down the back of the neck and then slide your fingers straight in under the ears. Feel for the occipital bones jutting out at the base of the skull, and the sharp corner of the jaw, known as the mastoid process, where the jaw muscles attach to the bone. Move your fingers along the bottom edge of the jaw toward the chin to feel the jaw bone. (Some rabbits will resist you touching them under the chin.)

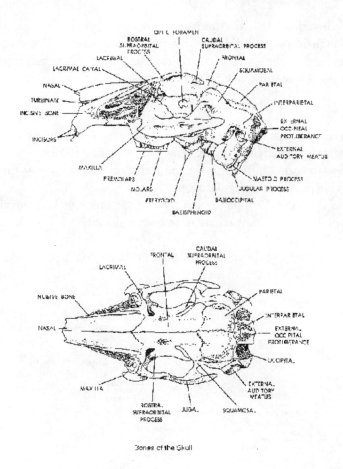

Bones of the Skull

The Spine

From the base of the neck, place your thumb and forefinger along either side of the spine and feel the bony vertebrae of the spinal column. Rabbits have seven cervical (neck) vertebrae, twelve thoracic (torso) vertebrae, and seven lumbar (lower back) vertebrae. These bones protect the spinal cord and get larger as you move from the neck toward the pelvis. Gently feel the depressions along the outer edges of the spine. The spokes that branch out of each vertebra are called the transverse processes, and the ridge at the top of each vertebra is the spinous process. You should never place direct pressure on these bony points. However, it is okay to use gentle pressure in the depressions between the transverse processes, squeezing the pressure points. An extensive network of nerves branches out from between each vertebra that are stimulated this way. There is also a group of long muscles (longissimus, multifidis) that reach from the neck all the way to the sacrum, connecting the spinal vertebrae together. Most all animals enjoy having these long paraspinal muscles massaged.

Scapulae and Front Limbs

Rabbits have triangular shoulder blades (scapulae) just like humans, except theirs lie horizontal to the body to support weight on their front limbs.

Find the top corner of the scapula and feel its outline with your fingers. You should be able to trace a triangular shape.

Next feel down to the shoulder joint, along the humerus bone, to the elbow joint. The point of the elbow is easy to feel when the rabbit is lying in the "loaf" position on its forepaws.

Gently feel the down the thin radius and ulna bones to the paw, and notice the tiny bones and joints in the forepaws.

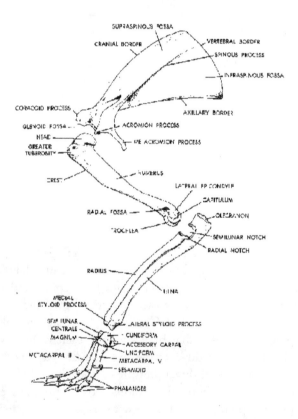

Ribs

Lay your hands on either side of your bunny with your wrists touching over the spine and your fingers pointing down. Beginning just below the edge of the scapula, use loose fingers to feel the ribs curving around the body. The ribs connect to the spinal vertebrae and to the front side of the body at the sternum. Focus on the fleshy area *between* the long rib bones, letting your fingers naturally fall into the grooves.

Pelvis

When a rabbit is sitting on its haunches, its leg will form a beautiful curve at the top. This is the iliac crest and the top edge of the pelvic bone. Your own iliac crest is easy to find. Many of us jut this bone out to carry children on our hip or balance a sack of groceries.

Feel for the large femur bone in the thigh, the patella over the knee joint, the tibia of the lower leg, down to the ankle joint and foot. Notice, too, all the small bones in the feet. The heel bone (calcaneus) is usually prominent on rabbits of all breeds.

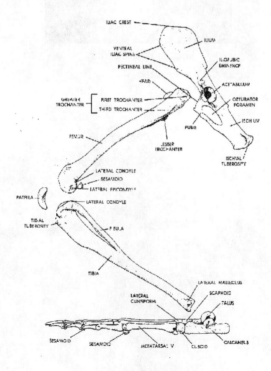

Bones of the Hindlimb

When you slide your fingers down a rabbit's back toward the tail, moving right along the edges of the spine, you'll come to a bony ridge between the hips where your fingers will naturally stop. This is the top of the sacrum. The sacrum is actually four bones fused together, developed over eons of evolution. It will feel like an inverted triangle with scalloped edges. Trace your fingers along the edges and feel for natural depressions along the sides. These are pressure points and also hold an array of nerve bundles.

When you reach the tip of the sacrum, keep going down to the tip of the tail and feel the tiny vertebrae in the rabbit's tail.

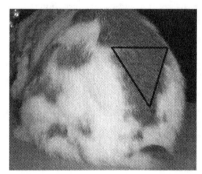

Locating the Sacrum

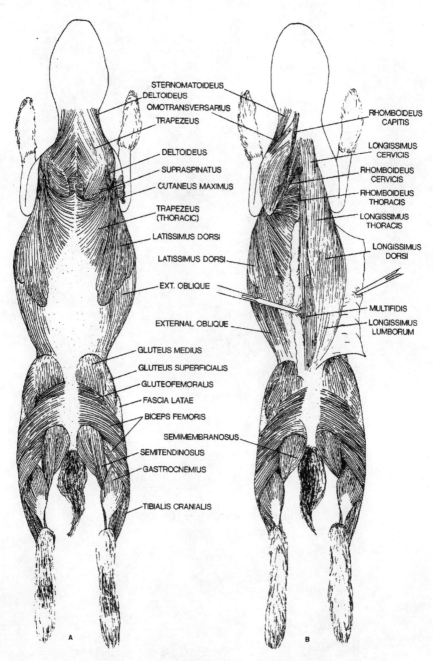

STERNOMATOIDEUS
DELTOIDEUS
OMOTRANSVERSARIUS
TRAPEZEUS

RHOMBOIDEUS
CAPITIS

DELTOIDEUS
SUPRASPINATUS
CUTANEUS MAXIMUS
TRAPEZEUS
(THORACIC)
LATISSIMUS DORSI

LONGISSIMUS
CERVICIS
RHOMBOIDEUS
CERVICIS
RHOMBOIDEUS
THORACIS
LONGISSIMUS
THORACIS

LATISSIMUS DORSI

LONGISSIMUS
DORSI

EXT. OBLIQUE

EXTERNAL OBLIQUE

MULTIFIDIS
LONGISSIMUS
LUMBORUM

GLUTEUS MEDIUS
GLUTEUS SUPERFICIALIS
GLUTEOFEMORALIS
FASCIA LATAE
BICEPS FEMORIS
SEMIMEMBRANOSUS
SEMITENDINOSUS
GASTROCNEMIUS

TIBIALIS CRANIALIS

A

B

Major Muscles of the Back (Dorsal View)

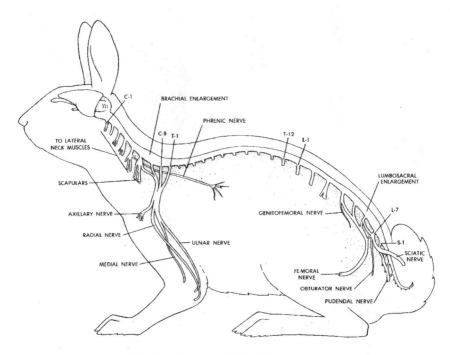

Major Nerves of the Rabbit

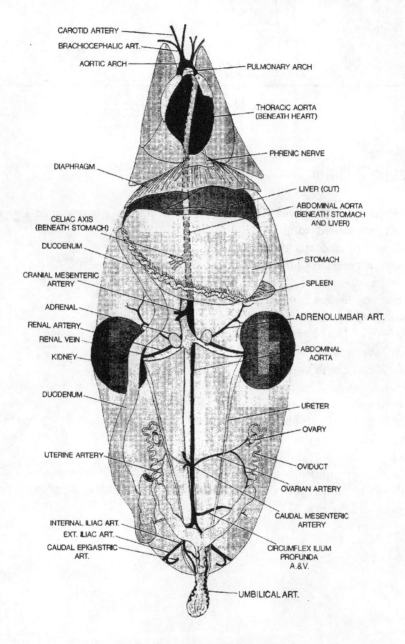

Major Organs of the Rabbit

Avoid direct pressure over organs and arteries.

CHAPTER 3

The Basic Strokes

Resting Position

The resting position allows your rabbit to become acclimated to the proximity of another being and sets the stage for the massage experience. This is the initial contact between two beings. You are entering another creature's personal space. Approach with respect.

Rest your hands gently on your pet's back. Take a deep breath. Relax your hands. Breathe with your pet. Stay in this position for about 15 seconds or until you feel centered and ready to begin.

Pausing at intervals during the massage and returning to the resting position allows the body to assimilate and process all the sensory input it has received. Rest briefly when finished with one area before moving on to the next.

Resting Position

Rocking

Rocking produces entrainment, the synchronization of two life rhythms. Breathing together and moving rhythmically instills a sense of calm and relaxation. Rocking begins with a gentle nudge, initiating a wave of movement through the whole body.

Place your palms on either side of your pet. Using one hand, push *gently* into the body and let the body swing out as far it wants to go naturally. Then let it swing back to the starting position. Use your opposite hand to stabilize but don't push back. Repeat until you produce a rhythmic back and forth movement.

Rocking

Effleurage

Effleurage is a French word meaning long, gliding strokes. This stroke prepares the body for deeper work by warming up the muscles. It is good for evaluating the quality of your pet's tissue, and feeling for areas of tension and gauging the tone of the muscle. Effleurage is also a nice stroke for transitioning from one area to another.

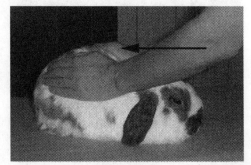

Effleurage

Effleurage can be done with the palms, fingertips, knuckles, or loose fists. Always use long, slow, broad strokes. Repeat the stroke several times, gradually increasing pressure. On the return stroke, release the pressure and mold your hands around the body part as you move back to your starting position.

Slow, lightweight effleurage has a reflexive effect and will often soothe a bunny to sleep. It is a sedating, calming stroke. Deeper effleurage using a slow speed is mechanical in effect, good for working out tense muscles. Faster effleurage strokes are stimulating and energizing.

Petrissage

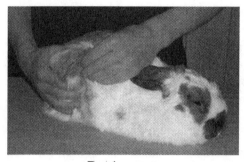

Petrissage is also borrowed from the French for "kneading." Petrissage is excellent for releasing tension directly from the muscles. It warms the tissue, making tendons more pliable and freeing adhesions. It nourishes tissue through increased circulation and helps remove metabolic waste, thus preventing stiffness after exercise. Petrissage also tones muscle by creating a contraction and release of the fibers, similar to what takes place during exercise.

Petrissage

Begin by making a "C" shape with each hand. Grasp the belly of the muscle—the meatiest part—and lift it away from the bone. Roll and squeeze it between your hands, then release. Use rhythmic movements pushing your hands toward one another, like kneading bread.

Compression

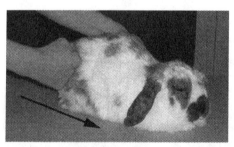

Compression employs steady, downward pressure with the fist, the heel of the hand, the thumb, or fingers. Customize this stroke to the size of the rabbit. Compression with the fist would not be appropriate for a dwarf rabbit, for example.

This action separates the muscle fibers as they are pressed against the bone. Compression releases adhesions and increases circulation. It is especially helpful when working with large muscle groups such as the hip or shoulder. Compression is also useful with ticklish rabbits or those with very long coats.

Compression

Skin Rolling

Skin rolling picks up the skin off the muscle and rolls it away from you as you move your hands. It is like petrissage but lifts only the skin layer away from the underlying muscle, rather than the muscle from the bone. Skin rolling warms and softens the connective tissue surrounding muscles, and is good for assessing an animal's tissue. "Stuck" skin that doesn't move freely often suggests underlying problems with the muscles. It is one stroke that can be done safely over the spine.

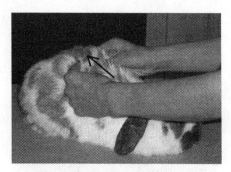

Skin Rolling

Pick up the skin using the thumbs and first two fingers, as if you were going to do finger petrissage. Now roll the skin between your fingers pushing gently away from your body. This stroke is similar to the Tellington Touch move (see more on TTouch below) called "tarantula pulling the plow."

Vibration

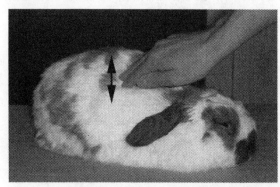

Vibration Hand Position

Vibration is a quick little stroke that can help break up the massage routine and wake up the nerves.

Begin with light compression into the muscle and then tremble your hand, vibrating it back and forth. Relax the muscles in your arm above the elbow. Allow the tissue to vibrate under your hand while maintaining contact and slight pressure. Vibration is great over muscle spasms or down either side of the spine.

Friction

Friction uses small, short rubbing movements against the grain of the muscle. It is useful around joints and bones where tendons and muscles attach, and over scar tissue. Friction is excellent for breaking up adhesions, but should never be done over a fresh injury. After proper healing, friction can help prevent the formation of scar tissue.

Hold your fingers together straight. Find the edge of the area of tension and use a fast rubbing motion across the muscle fibers. This is similar to vibration but works deeper in the muscle tissue.

Tapotement

Tapotement means "to rap, drum, or pat." It uses fast, springy taps on the body. This is the "karate chop" move you see in the movies. Tapotement is stimulating and works by activating the nerves. It's also effective on extremely tight muscles as it will "confuse" the muscles and nerves into letting go. With tapotement the body receives information than it can't organize quickly enough, so it goes slack.

Keep your hands and wrists relaxed, and use a fast drumming action, alternating your hands. Since most rabbits are small, you should use only the tips of your fingers in a tapping motion, or the inside part of your index fingers, as if you were playing a tiny drum. Never use tapotement directly over any endangerment site, bones, or organs.

Tellington Touch

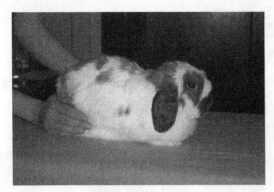

Tellington Touch

I also like to use Linda Tellington-Jones's wonderful TTouch technique. Her basic stroke is a circular motion using the hand. Visualize the face of a clock on your pet about an inch wide. Support the animal on one side with one hand. Slightly curve the fingers of your other hand and place them at six o'clock. Push with even pressure in a clockwise circle, coming all the way around past six o'clock to eight o'clock. Pause, then release your fingers softly and begin again in a new spot. Press only deeply enough to move the skin over the muscle. Randomly placed TTouch circles seem to help calm agitated animals.

CHAPTER 4

A Basic Massage Routine

Here is a simple massage routine that involves the whole body, and is great for maintaining health and inducing relaxation. You are by no means bound to follow this sequence every time you massage your pet. Use this as a starting point for learning the techniques and getting to know your rabbit's body. Later you can focus on specific areas of tension or rehabilitation, and develop your own moves. Listen to your pet's body with your hands.

You can work on the floor, on a table, in your lap, or wherever your rabbit is most comfortable.

Beginning the Session

Begin sitting so that you're facing your pet's side. Start with a light touch in the resting position. Slow your breathing and focus your attention on your pet. If the animal is agitated, do some informal petting first and let them settle down in a relaxed position.

Try some gentle rocking from side to side, letting the body swing only as far as it wants to go. Later, when you are both accustomed to this move, try rocking the body by holding the sides of the sacrum and initiating a movement up through the spine.

With a relaxed hand, begin light effleurage strokes from the nose, across the top of the skull to the base of the neck, and down the sides of the body. Stroke all the way to the end of the tail. Repeat this stroke using a little more pressure each time. Curve your hands at the start so that your fingers stroke across the big cheek muscles and your thumbs slide across the skull. Repeat this long stroke using circles over the muscles on either side of the spine.

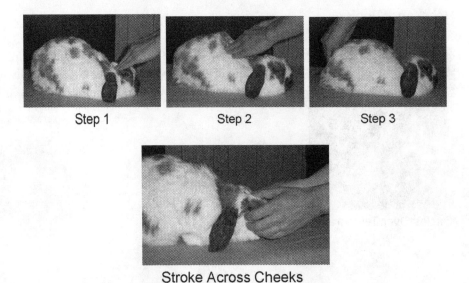

Step 1   Step 2   Step 3

Stroke Across Cheeks

Starting at the base of the skull, locate the depressions between the transverse processes of the spinal vertebrae. Press into these points as if your fingers could meet in the center of the spine. Do this all the way down the back, including the sacrum and ending at the tail.

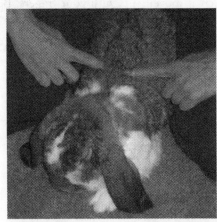

Pressing Points Along Spine

Head and Neck

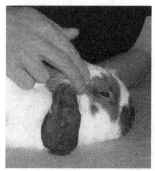

Make tiny circles with your fingers or thumbs up the bridge of the nose and around the temporalis muscle between the eyes and the base of the ears.

Circles Over Temporalis

Feel for the cartilaginous tissue around the base of the ear where it connects to the skull. Massage all around the base of the ear using circular movements with your fingers. Be sure to do both sides.

Massage Base of Ear

Rabbits have a large "masseter" muscle in their cheeks so they can powerfully chew and gnaw. Make tiny but deep circles all over the masseters, then stroke with your fingers from the chin to ear making your pet appear to grin.

Make Circles Over Masseters

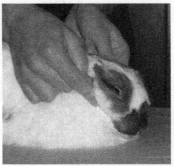

Grin

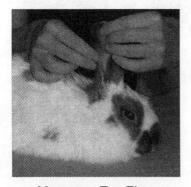

Massage Ear Flap

Hold the outer edge of the ear between your thumb and fingers with one hand and massage all along the flap with the other, beginning at the base and moving out to the tip. Use a circular motion like you would to feel the quality of fabric. This stimulates numerous acupressure points in the ear, and most rabbits enjoy having their ears rubbed. Be gentle, though; ears are delicate.

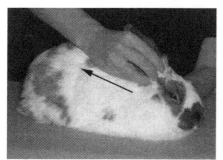

Gently Stretch the Ear From the Base

Grasp the base of the ear with your fingers and thumb and pull gently, stretching the ear away from the body. <u>Don't</u> pull from the soft flap or the tips of the ears. Repeat sequence on the other ear.

Change positions so that you are facing the back of your rabbit's head. Make a "C" with your hand and use your thumb and first two fingers to massage down the back of the neck to the shoulders. Rabbits have short necks, but feel with your fingers for the space between the skull and shoulders, then rub in circles with your fingers. There is a large nerve plexus between the shoulders that is stimulated with this stroke.

Make a "C" with your hand

Neck Massage

Shoulders and Forelegs

Circles Over Scapula

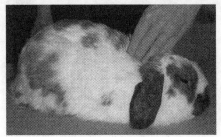

Fingers Behind Scapula

With the flats of your fingers, massage the outer muscles covering the shoulder blades using circles.

Find the edge of the scapula closest to the spine and sink your fingers down into the muscles behind the scapula. Reach in only as far as your rabbit will allow comfortably. Trace the edge of the scapula with your fingers. Feel for knots and tension in here and work them out with small fingertip circles or light compression. Rabbits tend to hold tension between their shoulders just as people do.

Starting at the top of the shoulder, make long passes with your whole hand down the foreleg to the foot. Rabbits are small enough that you could also mold your whole hand down the leg, then squeeze lightly and pull down, as if you were milking the legs. Repeat the sequence from shoulder to foot using petrissage.

Move down to the webbing between the toes. Hold the paw slightly off the table in your hand. Spread the toes apart gently by squeezing the flap of skin in between them. Repeat the entire sequence on the other leg. (Alternative: Hold your rabbit like an infant and work the legs and paws from this angle.)

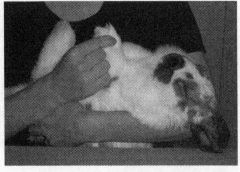

A Variation on Spreading the Toes

Thorax

Facing the side of your rabbit, reach across the opposite side with one hand so your fingertips touch the table or floor. Pull upward toward your body with curved fingers. Repeat this with the other hand, overlapping the area you just covered. Repeat by rapidly alternating your hands, moving down the side of the rabbit and back up to the shoulders. This is a comforting stroke called "wringing."

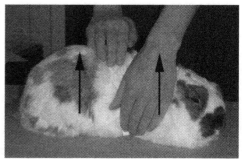

Wringing

Now fan your fingers apart and find the muscles between the ribs, the intercostals. Stroke down these muscles toward the belly and back up toward the spine.

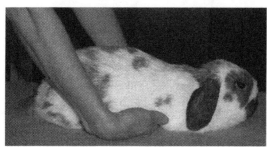

Tummy Lift Start Position

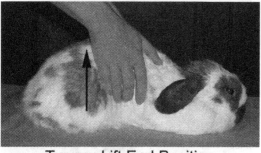

Tummy Lift End Position

With a hand on either side of the bunny, reach gently underneath the bun so that your fingertips meet under the stomach, just below the sternum and ribs. Gently slide your hands upward, slightly lifting the tummy. Repeat 3-4 times, gently working from the sternum down toward the tail. This is a great technique for relieving gas.

If your rabbit is comfortable on their back in your arms, you could also massage their abdomen with gentle circles using your fingers.

Facing the back of your rabbit's head, reach around the front to work the pectoral muscles on the chest. Let your fingertips meet under the chin, below the neck, over the sternum. Pull your hands backward, spreading the pectorals apart with your fingers.

Hand Position for Pectoral Spread

Fingers Meet Over the Chest

Pull Pectoral Muscles Toward Tail

Hips and Hind Legs

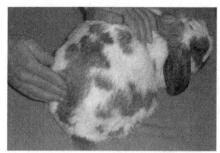

Circles Over the Sacrum

Locate the sacrum and make broad circles over the surface with your fingers or the heel of your hand. Press your fingers gently into the pressure points around the outer edges of the sacrum. Press inward as though your fingertips could meet in the center. Some rabbits are sensitive here. Watch for feedback.

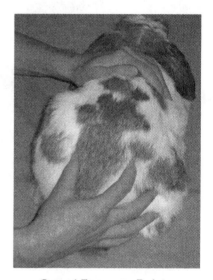

Sacral Pressure Points

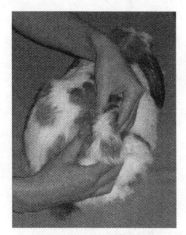

Petrissage Over Hips

Using petrissage, knead the large muscles covering the hips. Work from the iliac crest down to the foot. If your rabbit is lying on her stomach with her legs outstretched, and is comfortable with you working on her legs, knead the large gastrocnemius (calf) muscle on the back of the leg, and the Achilles tendon down to the ankle. Also work around the kneecap using tiny friction. Spread the toes apart as you did on the forepaws. (Many rabbits are "foot shy" or ticklish on their feet. Even after six years of massage, I only get to work on Maia's calves and feet on occasion because she is sensitive here.)

Gently massage the tail, then grasp it with your fingers and give it a *slight* stretch outward.

Finish the massage with some light, full body effleurage, stroking from the nose to the tail. Sit quietly with your rabbit for a few minutes to let the effects of the massage sink in.

Tail Pull

Variations

It can sometimes be difficult to thoroughly work the front and back limbs. All rabbits have different levels of touch tolerance. When rabbits are in the loaf position, they tuck their legs under them, making them difficult to access. You can perform the same strokes on the limbs by holding your rabbit on its back like an infant. Support their body with one hand and hug them snugly against your torso. Use your free hand to massage one limb at a time. Only do this if your rabbit is comfortable in this position! If they find it stressful to begin with, they will not appreciate your massage. You know your rabbit best. Respect their needs and find ways to massage comfortably for you both.

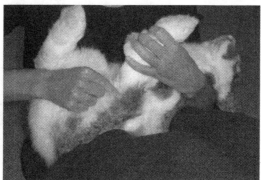

Massaging the Calf Muscle

CHAPTER 5

Special Cases

Wry Neck/Head Tilt

Some rabbits develop head tilt, also called torticolis, from inner ear infections or the parasite *e. cuniculi*, and occasionally from a stroke or trauma. These infections give the rabbit a sense of vertigo, and they can't figure out which way is up. It must feel like being very drunk when the room spins around you! Their neck muscles then adapt to keeping the head turned sideways. It is essential to treat any of these conditions immediately. Some rabbits never regain their balance even after the infection clears up because their muscles have adapted to the new position.

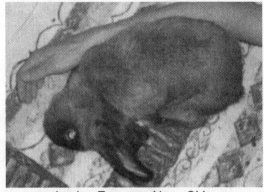
Laying Forearm Along Side

Massage can help rabbits recovering from head tilt. Massage alters the body's positional sense and initiates specific movement patterns that change sensory input from muscles, tendons, joints, and the skin. This feedback information, which adjusts and coordinates movement, is relayed directly to the motor cortex and the cerebellum. A rabbit's sense of which way is up and its righting reflex are located in the cerebellum. The vestibular apparatus of the inner ear, responsible for balance mechanism, and the cerebellum are interrelated. Massage stimulates the cerebellum by altering muscle tone and position, and in turn the vestibular balance stimulates the hypothalamus to adjust automatic nervous system functions to restore homeostasis.

The techniques that most strongly affect the vestibular apparatus and therefore the cerebellum are those that produce rhythmic rocking. Rocking produces movement at the neck and head that influences the sense of equilibrium, and stimulates the inner ear balance mechanisms to keep the head level. Pressure on the sides of the body may also stimulate the body-righting reflex. Stimulation of this reflex produces a body-wide effect involving stimulation of muscle contraction patterns that pass throughout the body.

For these rabbits, hunker over them and place your forearm along the side of the body that the rabbit is "looking" away from. Notice how they lean against your arm with the muscles alongside their body. Hold your arm in place, then gently release and repeat. Contraction of the muscles opposite the tilt can help right your rabbit's sense of balance.

You may also try gentle rocking movements around the head and neck, or using your whole forearm with the exercise above. Let the movement be natural and soft. Rock for about 30 seconds, then rest with your hands still but maintain contact. Repeat.

Geriatric Bunnies

Rabbits are subject to the ravages of time like all living creatures. Muscle tissue diminishes as we age and is replaced by fat and connective tissue, making it less pliable. Older rabbits have thinner skin, and their circulation slows down. Regular massage can help counteract the effects of aging. A general relaxation routine will go a long way.

Any gentle petrissage or small fingertip circles are good for rabbits who are already advanced in age. Be sure to work around their joints where the muscles attach to the bone. If they'll allow you to, hold the joint in your hand and take the limb through the normal range of motion to keep the joint mobile. Support them by ensuring that they drink plenty of water.

GI Stasis

Gastrointestinal stasis is unfortunately common in house rabbits. Too many treats and too little exercise can result in bloated tummies. If your rabbit is having abdominal distress, first see a veterinarian to determine the cause. I cannot emphasize this point enough! Massage may be contraindicated if there is a risk of dislodging a blockage or rupturing the gut, and could prove fatal to your rabbit. If your rabbit suffers from gas or mild discomfort, and with your vet's approval, light tummy rubs are appropriate.

You can use the tummy lifts described herein. Start just under the sternum and repeat the lifting motion as you work down the abdomen toward the tail. Work very gently and slowly. You will probably hear a lot of gurgling from your bunny's tummy, or feel masses of gas or digestive matter moving through their intestines. Let them hop away when they are ready and they will probably empty their bowels.

You can also perform small circular effleurage with your fingertips or the flat of your hand by holding your rabbit like an infant and rubbing in a clockwise motion over the tummy.

Molar Spurs and Malocclusion

Rabbits with teeth problems can develop sore cheek muscles and neck muscles from different patterns of chewing, or from having their jaws forced open to have their molars floated. Most rabbits love to have their masseter muscles rubbed anyway.

Find the large cheek muscle and feel the fibers running vertically. This arrangement of the fibers is what makes this muscle so strong. Stroke across the fibers with your fingers like a harp, then massage the whole muscle with fingertip circles. Massage the edge of the jaw bone from the chin back to the neck. Then rub the neck muscles down to the shoulders. If your rabbit will let you, stretch the neck muscles by holding the head under the ears and pressing the shoulders in the opposite direction.

Deaf or Blind

Rabbits who are hearing or visually impaired still respond to touch stimulus. Touch can be comforting and help a blind rabbit orient themselves in space. Any sort of general relaxation massage will help these rabbits function well. Rocking, too, will help blind rabbits. Deaf rabbits have the same needs as other rabbits, and a basic massage sequence will help support their entire system.

Paralysis

Increased circulation is especially important for these critters, and massage can help the flow of blood and lymph through the body. Immobility can lead to atrophied tissue and a lack of interest in life. Even when a rabbit has lost the use of a limb, increasing the circulation to that area can help maintain healthy tissue. It feels good and raises their awareness of the rest of their body. Accepting a disability and adapting to new routines in life can be stressful for any species. Massage supports their overall health and can help a disabled rabbit live a happy life.

When Your Rabbit Just Says No

There are rabbits out there who, whether by personality or past experience, just don't trust massage and will refuse touch. To make progress with these guys, plan to spend a lot of time earning trust. Begin by just sitting quietly in the same room, perhaps reading a book, and let the rabbit do whatever they want—check you out, hide from you, etc. Don't make any attempts at contact unless they initiate. Lie down on their level and let your hands rest on the floor. If they come over to sniff your fingers, try a brief resting position on them. Gradually begin to incorporate strokes.

There is a lot of energy concentrated in the palm of the human hand and this can feel overwhelming to sensitive creatures. Try using the back of your hand for the first contact. You could also build an artificial arm and hand from a broomstick and an old glove. Use this to get your rabbit used to feeling non-threatening pressure against its body.

Alternately, try "beaming" energy across the room to your rabbit. Hold your palms in their direction and imagine a golden light coming into the top of your head and out your palms. Visualize it surrounding the rabbit. Take deep breaths. Sometimes energy work can lay the foundation for physical touch.

EPILOGUE

Maia crossed over the Rainbow Bridge before this book went to print. She died from complications arising from a dislocated hip. Her death was a shock to everyone, and we miss her greatly. But her contributions to my life and the lives of others go beyond any physical boundaries of time and space. She will always be my inspiration, teacher, and guide. May her blessings extend to you and your bunnies.

ABOUT THE AUTHORS

Chandra Moira Beal, RMT

Chandra Moira Beal is a registered massage therapist and a freelance writer in Austin, Texas. She spends her days writing articles and books, teaching, volunteering with numerous animal welfare organizations, and providing massage and Reiki to people and pets. Her life is a joyful blend of communicating, healing, and playing. She shared her home with Maia for six years. Chandra is also the author of *Splash Across Texas! The Definitive Guide to Swimming in Central Texas* and *The Santa Cruz Beach Boardwalk: Never a Dull Moment*. To learn more, visit www.beal-net.com/laluna.

Maia

Maia was a brown and white tortoiseshell mini-lop who lived 1997-2003. She had free run of a large house, which she dutifully protected. She toured schools giving presentations on humane education, and wrote her own column on animal massage in a quarterly newsletter. Maia inspired many articles, including an appearance in Rabbits USA 2003, and had pen pals around the world. She volunteered as a greeter rabbit at House Rabbit Resource Network meetings, and as a "demo" bunny at pet adoption days. She assisted with Reiki sessions and supervised massage. Maia was part wise sage, part court jester. Above all, she was Chandra's best friend.

BIBLIOGRAPHY & RESOURCES

Bibliography

Fox, Michael DVM. <u>The Healing Touch</u>, Newmarket Press, 1981

Fritz, Sandy. <u>Mosby's Fundamentals of Therapeutic Massage</u>, Mosby, Inc., 2000

Harriman, Marinell. <u>House Rabbit Handbook</u>, Drollery Press, 1995.

McLaughlin, Charles A. and Robert B. Chiasson. <u>Laboratory Anatomy of the Rabbit</u>, McGraw Hill, 1970

Schwartz, Cheryl, DVM. <u>Four Paws, Five Directions</u>, Celestial Arts, 1996

Smith, Kathy. <u>Rabbit Health in the 21st Century</u>, 2nd Edition, iUniverse, 2003

Tellington-Jones, Linda. <u>The Tellington Touch</u>, Penguin Books, 1992

Rabbit Resources

House Rabbit Society
<u>www.rabbit.org</u>

House Rabbit Resource Network
<u>www.rabbitresource.org</u>

Chandra's Rabbit Web Site
<u>www.beal-net.com/chandra/rabbits</u>

0-595-31062-1

CPSIA information can be obtained
at www.ICGtesting.com
Printed in the USA
LVHW092219210421
685204LV00005B/281